DICKENS
AND THE
VICTORIANS

Stewart Ross

Illustrated by Gerry Wood

Wayland

LIFE AND TIMES

First published in 1986 by
Wayland (Publishers) Ltd
61 Western Road, Hove
East Sussex BN3 1JD, England

© Copyright 1986 Wayland (Publishers) Ltd

**British Library Cataloguing in
Publication Data**
Ross, Stewart
Dickens and the Victorians. — (Life and times)
1. Great Britain — History — Victoria, 1837-1901
— Juvenile literature.
I. Title   II. Wood, Gerald, 1938-   III. Series
941.081   DA551

ISBN 0-85078-620-7

Phototypeset by Planagraphic Typesetters Ltd
Printed in Italy by G. Canale & C.S.p.A., Turin
Bound in Great Britain at The Bath Press, Avon

Contents

1 CHARLES DICKENS

The great entertainer

In the autumn of 1858 a new craze swept across Britain. From Plymouth to Edinburgh, people filled halls and theatres to hear a popular writer of the day read extracts from his work. Every performance was sold out. Audiences roared with laughter, shouted with pleasure and even wept with sorrow. The man who gave the readings knew how to control his listeners, for he was also a successful amateur actor. His name was Charles Dickens.

Dickens was born in 1812, the second of eight children. His father, John Dickens, was a clerk. He was hopeless at organizing the family money and always spent too much. In 1824 he was arrested for debt and sent to the Marshalsea prison for debtors in London. His family, except for Charles, went with him. Aged only twelve, Charles had to earn a meagre living by sticking labels on to pots of blacking. It was an experience he never forgot. He was determined to do well for himself, and to put the poverty and shame of his childhood as far behind him as possible.

From an early age it was clear that Charles Dickens had a talent for writing. When he was fifteen he gained employment as a clerk in a lawyer's office, but a year later he left this job to become a newspaper reporter. By 1832 he was reporting Parliamentary debates and by the time he was twenty-four, he had started his first novel, *The Pickwick Papers*. It was to prove a remarkable success.

Above *Dickens loved to perform scenes from his books, no matter how small the audience.*

Below *One of Dickens's most popular creations, Mr Pickwick.*

Right *Charles's boyhood experience of poverty and factory work greatly influenced his attitudes to the plight of the poor and of working children.*

Above *Dickens was a prolific writer and one of great imaginative power.*

The novelist

Charles Dickens is possibly the most popular English novelist. In every corner of the world his books are read, or seen as plays, films or musicals. After *The Pickwick Papers* he wrote *Oliver Twist*. Thirteen successful novels followed, including *David Copperfield,* which was based on his early life.

The novels were published in serial form, month by month. Dickens wrote one episode at a time, altering the plot to suit the tastes of his readers, a method which caused his books to be rather long and rambling. However, their popularity lay more in the characters he created than the stories themselves.

Below *A scene from* Oliver Twist: *Oliver (right) is introduced to the evil old pickpocket, Fagin.*

The people in Dickens's novels are larger than life. He exaggerates certain aspects of their personalities, making them like cartoon characters. There is Scrooge the miser, Bill Sykes the villain, and Mr. Micawber, who is always waiting for something to turn up — just like Dickens's father. Dickens created a whole world of his own in the pages of his novels.

In 1858, when he began his tour of public readings, Dickens was separated from his wife, Catherine. Their marriage was not a happy one, and Charles now put more and more energy into his public appearances. His friends said that the strain of this work hastened the end, for he died of a stroke on 8th June 1870, aged only 58.

Below *When he toured the United States, in November 1867, Dickens's public readings met with similar acclaim to that received in Britain.*

The reformer

Dickens was a campaigner for social reform. He realized that there was much wrong with nineteenth-century society and he expressed his opinions through the characters of his novels. Even in *The Pickwick Papers*, a lighthearted work, he drew a sinister picture of the inside of the Fleet prison for debtors. When the kind Mr. Pickwick entered the prison, he could not believe what he saw. 'My friend,' he said, 'you don't really mean to say that human beings live down in those wretched dungeons?'

In 1842 Dickens visited the United States. He was horrified at the slavery he found there, and in his next novel, *Martin Chuzzlewit*, he bitterly attacked this feature of American life. Back in England, he helped to set up a home where prostitutes could start new lives. He also campaigned for the abolition of capital punishment and the reform of Parliament.

Above *Nicholas Nickleby takes revenge on the cruel Wackford Squeers.*

Dickens felt strongly about the state of education in Britain. In several of his books he describes bad schools, run by wicked or misguided masters. The most famous is Dotheboys Hall, in *Nicholas Nickleby*. After working for a while with the headmaster, Mr. Wackford Squeers, Nicholas can stand his bullying no longer, and so he beats Mr. Squeers with his own cane in front of the class. How Dickens's audience must have roared with delight when this passage was read to them.

At Dickens's funeral a cabman was heard to say, 'Ah, Mr. Dickens was a great man, and a true friend of the poor.' Indeed he was.

Below *Dickens's description of the awful conditions in Fleet Prison was an early example of social protest in his writing.*

2 VICTORIA, ALBERT AND THE UPPER CLASS

The Royal Family

Above *Victoria married Prince Albert, who came from the German state of Saxe-Coburg-Gotha, in 1840.*

Below *Victoria mourned Albert's death in isolation for such a long period that she became known as the 'Widow of Windsor'.*

Shortly before his death, Dickens was given the great honour of being introduced to Queen Victoria. At the end of their ninety-minute meeting he gave the Queen a set of his works and, in exchange, she presented him with a copy of her *Journal of Our Life in the Highlands*.

Victoria was a remarkable woman. She came to the throne in 1837, aged eighteen. By the time she died, in 1901, she had won the hearts of her subjects in every corner of the British Empire. Her nine children had married into many of the ruling families of Europe, and she was known as the 'grandmother of Europe'.

At first, Victoria relied heavily upon her wise and intelligent German husband, Prince Albert. He did much for Britain, and will always be remembered for his role in organizing the Great Exhibition of 1851. The Queen was heartbroken by Albert's early death in 1861. Her grief led her to withdraw from public life for several years.

In the 1870s, Victoria began to appear in public once more. She was learning not to interfere in politics and to keep her strongest personal feelings to herself. By the time of her death she had done much to ensure the popularity of the monarchy and she had given her name to the age in which she lived.

Right *Victoria is informed that, at the age of eighteen, she is to be Queen.*

12

The upper class

Social class was very important to the Victorians. Most people belonged to the working class, the majority of others were middle class, and a tiny percentage were members of the upper class or aristocracy.

There were about 300 British aristocratic families, most of whom had incomes of more than £100,000 a year (enough to make a millionaire in today's money). Some of them were related to the Queen. They did not need to work because they had inherited money and land from their ancestors. They lived on huge estates in the country, such as Blenheim Palace in Oxfordshire (where Winston Churchill was born) and they also owned houses in London. Most of the families had a great sense of responsibility and service, making use of their privileged position sensibly. A few were less responsible. Dickens was quick to criticize such people, as he did in his portrayal of Lord Frederick Verisopht, a young fop, in *Nicholas Nickleby*.

The gentry were lower than the aristocracy on the social scale. They had incomes of about £1,000 a year and held many of the important positions in the country. They formed the majority of the membership of Parliament, and were officers in the army and navy, or clergymen.

The families of the aristocracy and gentry were a privileged class which controlled much of Britain's wealth and power. They employed numerous servants, had beautiful homes and fine clothes. The rest of Victorian Britain regarded them with a mixture of respect and envy.

Above *Wealthy Victorians relax at Henley Royal Regatta.*

Below *The fashionable gentry paid strict attention to dress and manner.*

Left *The Duke of Westminster employed no fewer than forty gardeners to tend the grounds surrounding his home at Eaton Hall.*

15

3 THE MIDDLE CLASS

Respectable people

The Dickens family looked upon themselves as middle class because John Dickens was employed as a clerk in the Navy Pay Office. When his father went to prison, the young Charles had to do manual work to earn his living. This was working-class employment, which is why Charles was so ashamed of it.

The Victorian middle class was respectable. They tried to speak with 'correct' accents and to wear fashionable clothes. They usually went to church on Sundays. All middle-class families kept servants to do the household work, such as cleaning, cooking, shopping and washing, because the middle class did not do any manual work.

It is not easy to define the boundaries of the middle class. It included wealthy businessmen, like Scrooge, in *A Christmas Carol,* who might earn as much as £1,000 a year; yet it also contained shopkeepers earning £50 a year. Doctors, lawyers and other well-paid professions formed the upper-middle class. Clerks like Scrooge's Bob Cratchit, were members of the lower-middle class.

During the reign of Queen Victoria, Britain became a much richer country. This new wealth helped to increase the size of the middle class, so that by 1900 about one-fifth of the population belonged to it. They included the thousands of new teachers, secretaries, civil servants and businessmen who so enjoyed Dickens's novels.

Below *For most middle-class families church attendance was of great importance.*

17

At home

The Victorian middle classes led strictly ordered lives. The father was definitely in charge of the household and wives were expected to obey their husbands. For much of the nineteenth century, the law required women to hand over all their wealth to their husbands when they married. The family relationships were so formal that children often called their fathers 'sir'. When parents could afford it, their children were brought up by nannies. As a result, they saw them only at meals and at bedtime. At meals, children were expected to be seen and not heard, except when they were spoken to. Manners were most important to the Victorian middle class.

Below *Friends gather around the piano to sing their favourite songs.*

Middle-class families enjoyed a good diet. They did not understand which foods were good for them and ate too much cream and butter. However, they also had plenty of meat and vegetables to eat. Many middle-class families didn't approve of drinking alcohol. They noticed the enormous amount of drunkenness among the lower classes and considered drinking to be disreputable.

The most popular family entertainment was an evening round the piano. Everyone joined in, playing or singing songs which we now regard as rather sentimental. People read a good deal, particularly as there were no such distractions as television or radio. Sometimes the family went to their theatre or to a concert, and in the summer it became fashionable to take a holiday at a seaside resort. By the end of the century both men and women took up many different sports in their free time and the wealthier families might have bought one of the first motor cars.

Above *A middle-class family enjoyed a good diet, each meal often consisting of at least four courses.*

Below *A father reads a bedtime story to his children.*

19

Above *In the city areas, the double rows of houses formed courtyards in which a lavatory and a water pump were placed. These would be used by the occupants of about twenty households.*

4 THE WORKERS

City dwellers

Queen Victoria's reign covered a period of very great change. Between 1837 and 1901, the population of Britain rose from 19 million to 37 million. At the same time an industrial revolution was taking place, changing the country from one in which most people lived in small towns and villages, into a nation of city dwellers. In 1801, Cardiff was little more than a large village, with a population of about 2,000. But, one hundred years later, 164,000 people lived in this great capital city.

In the expanding towns and cities, very little care was taken to see that new buildings were planned or constructed carefully. Hundreds of thousands of shoddy houses were built near factories to provide homes for the work-force. Rents were low, but the standard of housing was disgraceful. Buildings were very often damp and unhealthy, without running water, lighting, lavatories or drains. Families usually had to live in one room, where the air was thick with the smoke from the fires that burned in houses and factories all over the city. In *Dombey and Son* Dickens described with loathing 'a row of houses, with little squalid patches of ground before them, fenced off with old doors, barrel staves, scraps of tarpaulin, and dead bushes'.

Of course not all the poor lived in slums. Some employers, like George Cadbury, built excellent cottages for their workers. Yet millions of Victorians spent their lives in conditions which we would consider too bad even for animals.

Below *The unhealthy and overcrowded housing conditions encouraged the rapid spread of diseases such as pneumonia, tuberculosis and cholera.*

Employment

Above *A Victorian cartoon portraying the cruel exploitation of women.*

At the beginning of the nineteenth century there were almost no laws controlling employment. Men, women and children could work for any number of hours, in any conditions, for any wages. Young boys were employed as chimney sweeps, because they could climb up the inside of chimneys to clean them. Children were also put to work in coal mines, where their small size made them useful. Women worked as seamstresses in damp cellars for up to sixteen hours a day. Each year thousands of men and women were killed in accidents at work.

Right *Children drag heavily laden carts through the narrow shaft of a coal mine.*

Skilled workers, such as engineers, were quite well paid and led reasonably comfortable lives. The pay of unskilled labourers, however, was very low, as we saw with the young Charles Dickens. One pound a week was considered a good wage for a man. Families on such low incomes could not afford adequate food, so they were always undernourished. This, and poor housing, contributed to the high annual mortality rate. The average age of death in some parts of the country was as low as seventeen.

Over the Victorian period the living and working conditions of the working class improved. Laws were passed limiting the hours of work, and preventing the employment of women and children in unsuitable conditions. Wages went up, safety guards were placed on machinery and slums were cleared. By 1901, many workers still lived in poverty, but they were generally better off than their grandparents had been.

Above *Two young girls sift dust, from which bricks could be made.*

The underworld

Victorian cities were riddled with crime. *Oliver Twist* presents a lively picture of this underworld of vice, with thugs like Bill Sykes and the evil old pickpocket, Fagin.

Men, women and children wandered into the cities looking for work. If they were unsuccessful, they were faced with the dreadful prospect of turning to crime. Young Oliver Twist became involved with a gang of thieves in London without realizing it. In the ill-lit streets muggers were a constant danger. Dickens's novel, *Our Mutual Friend*, opens with two people making a living from fishing dead bodies out of the river Thames and robbing them.

Towards the end of the century terrorism became more common. In the nineteenth century the whole of Ireland was part of the United Kingdom and some Irish nationalists fought violently for independence. In 1882, two English politicians were hacked to death with surgical knives in Phoenix Park, Dublin by a secret group calling themselves the Invincibles. The nation was deeply shocked.

When Victoria came to the throne the Metropolitan Police (serving London) had recently been founded. In 1839, the system was extended to the rest of the country. Gradually the number of crimes for which a person could be executed was reduced, as punishments were made more humane. After 1853, for example, convicts could no longer be sent to Australia as a punishment. Detective work also improved — Sherlock Holmes was a Victorian creation — and slowly, as living standards improved, the ghastly Victorian underworld was cleaned up.

Above *The notorious schemer, Fagin, hatches another sinister plot.*

Below *The first uniformed police force was founded in London, in 1829, by Sir Robert Peel.*

Right *The backstreets of most Victorian cities were unsafe and were the haunt of thieves and robbers.*

In the country

Until the 1870s, British agriculture flourished. Farmers grew rich providing food for the growing population. At ten shillings (50p) a week, agricultural labourers were even more poorly paid than factory workers. Much of their work was back-breaking, and in the summer they worked from dawn to dusk. But they usually had a house provided with the job, and at least they worked in the fresh air, away from the dirt, crime and disease of the city.

During the last thirty years of the century, there was a slump in agriculture. There were several bad harvests and cheap corn was imported from the U.S.A. and Canada by steamship. Frozen meat came from Australia and New Zealand at prices British farmers could not match. Consequently, owners of large estates made labourers redundant, small farmers went bankrupt, and farm-hands sought work in the towns. In order to make farming more efficient, new machinery was introduced.

In one part of the British Isles the story of rural life was even more bleak. The main food of the Irish was the potato, but in 1845 a fungus destroyed the whole crop. The country was faced with starvation. The government in London was unable to cope with the disaster. As a result one million people died, and two million emigrated. Much of the land in Ireland was then owned by English landlords, and consequently Irish hatred of them grew. Throughout the rest of the nineteenth century much of Ireland remained a poor, backward agricultural society, governed by despised English Protestant masters.

Above *The number of farm labourers declined rapidly during the Victorian era.*

Below *The introduction of mechanized farming led to greater efficiency in food production.*

Right *An Irish family is evicted during the Irish potato famine.*

26

5 THE AGE OF REFORM

Protest

'Government', wrote Thomas Duncombe in a Charter of 1842, 'was designed to protect the freedom and promote the happiness of . . . the whole people . . . Any form of government which fails (to do this) . . . is tyrannical, and ought to be amended or resisted.' Popular opinion agreed with Duncombe. Hundreds of campaigns were organized to persuade the government to do more for the people of Britain.

Above *One of the most urgent reforms demanded by the Chartists was the right to vote in secret. This was eventually granted in the Ballot Act of 1872.*

Right *Violent confrontations were common at demonstrations seeking reform during the 1830s and 1840s.*

28

The working class needed the benefits of reform the most. Their anger at the conditions they had to endure led to frequent outbreaks of rioting in the 1840s. In the first half of the century Parliament was presented with petitions (called Charters) which had been signed by thousands and demanded reforms, such as the vote for all men. Parliament rejected all of their proposals.

The working class met with more success by forming trade unions. By striking — as the London dockers discovered in 1889 — they improved wages. Finally, the Labour Party was formed in 1900 to represent the working class in Parliament.

Sometimes middle-class and working-class protesters worked together, as in the Anti-Corn Law League. Some of the middle-class reformers became MPs, while others, like Dickens, expressed their views in novels and newspapers. Clubs were formed, rallies organized, letters written. As a result of these efforts the later nineteenth century became known as an age of reform.

Above *The second Chartist petition is borne to Parliament in 1842.*

Political reform

For much of the nineteenth century the British people had little say in the way they were governed. Parliament was at the heart of politics but unlike today, it did not represent the wishes of the people. Women had no part in political life. In 1837, only about 500,000 wealthy men were permitted to vote, out of a total population of 25 million.

In *The Pickwick Papers* Dickens described an election at Eatanswill. In the name he chose for the town ('Eat — and — Swill') he was telling his readers what he thought of elections. Voting was not secret and the candidates tried to bribe the electors with food and drink. During the course of the century the method of election changed considerably. In 1832, just before Victoria became Queen,

Below *Until 1832 there were few laws governing the election of candidates for Parliament. Bribery and corruption were widespread.*

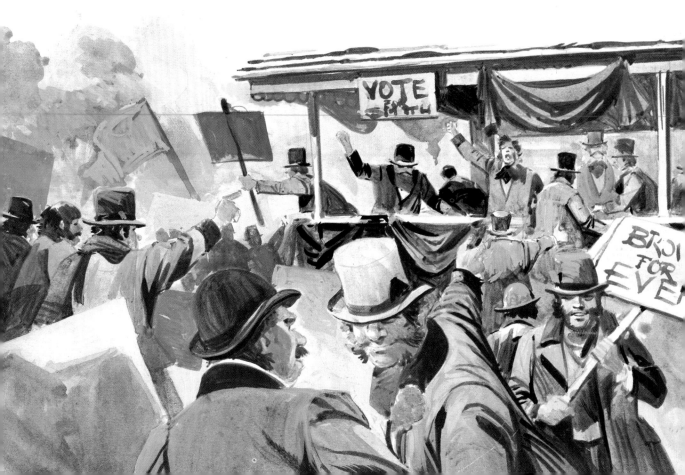

some constituencies had been made more representative, and more men had been given the vote. The process was taken further in 1867 and 1884/5. Voting was made secret in 1872. Local government was reformed in 1888 and 1894. By the time of the Queen's death, most men over twenty-one could vote in Parliamentary elections, but women were still not allowed to vote at all. It was a slow start, but Britain was on the road to democracy.

Two names are associated more than any others with Victorian reform: William Gladstone, four times the Liberal Prime Minister between 1868 and 1895; and Benjamin Disraeli, the Conservative leader between 1868 and 1881. Between them these two great statesmen spearheaded the drive for change.

Above *Benjamin Disraeli (top). William Gladstone (bottom).*

Above *Towards the end of the century, better housing equipped with decent facilities was provided in towns and cities.*

Social reform

In the early nineteenth century the government felt that it should interfere with people's lives as little as possible. There were harsh laws against crime, but there were few measures to protect citizens against cruelty or unfairness. In this society the rich flourished, while the poor suffered. They were supposed to help themselves.

The Victorian reformers made strenuous efforts to change this situation. Many new laws dealt with

employment. Children were protected from working in dangerous places or for long hours and a minimum age-level was set for those permitted to work. Dangerous machinery had to be fenced in, and compensation could be claimed by those injured at work. A ten-hour working day was established and factory inspectors were employed to see that the new regulations were obeyed.

The Government also tried to improve the nation's health. Minimum standards were established for housing, water supply and drains. City councils were given the right to clear slums. Pubs were licensed to open for limited hours each day, and the purity of food and drink on sale was protected by law.

The energy of the Victorians was amazing. There was hardly an aspect of life that they did not reform, from the safety of ships to street lighting.

Above *Laws were passed in the late nineteenth century to ensure the protection of industrial machinery and the insurance of employees against injury.*

Above *The entrance to the Crystal Palace.*

6 THE WEALTH OF THE NATION

The Crystal Palace

On 1st May 1851, a new building was opened in London's Hyde Park. Known as the Crystal Palace, it was like a huge greenhouse 563 metres (616 yards) long, 122 metres (133 yards) wide and 18 metres (20 yards) high. Some of the trees in the park were left to grow inside it. The Palace had been put up to house the Great Exhibition, in which all the latest developments in the industrial world were exhibited.

It was no coincidence that the Great Exhibition was held in London. At that time Britain was the wealthiest nation on earth, for she had been the first to have an 'Industrial Revolution'. During the course of the previous century the population had risen dramatically, from 7½ million to 25 million. Improved farming methods enabled the population to be fed. In addition, several new inventions, such as the power-loom for weaving, made factories necessary, and soon mass-produced goods were flooding into the shops.

British products were sold not only at home, but also in Europe and throughout the Empire. Railways and steamships were used to transport them swiftly and safely to their destinations.

As the Industrial Revolution advanced, more industries flourished. Coal mining, iron and steel manufacture, cloth production, shipping — there was hardly a branch of manufacture that was not growing. It is small wonder that Britain became known as the 'workshop of the world'.

Above *The size and scope of the Great Exhibition was breathtaking.*

New rivals

Above *Competition from abroad threatened Britain's agriculture as well as its industry. Here imported meat from Australia is being unloaded at the Albert Docks in 1897.*

Britain's leadership of the industrial world did not last long. By the time of Queen Victoria's death, several other countries had become industrialized and their output had overtaken that of Britain.

Germany only became a united country the year after Dickens's death, and the America which Martin Chuzzlewit (a character in one of Dickens's novels) visited was still an underdeveloped land. Yet, by the end of the century these two mighty nations, both with greater populations and greater natural resources than Britain, led the industrial world. They became industrialized later than Britain, and consequently the manufacturing processes and machinery they employed were more modern and efficient.

Some British industrialists were over-confident. They did not take much interest in new products, such as electrical goods or motor cars, and so foreign companies dominated. The German manfacturer Benz named one of his first cars after his daughter, Mercedes. It was a great success.

Money that could have been invested in British industry was used to finance projects abroad, such as the construction of railways in South America. Britain kept a policy of free trade, which meant that imports and exports could pass freely in and out of the country. Many other nations kept out British imports with high tariffs. In 1900 Britain was still a great world power and trading nation, but her age of supremacy had passed.

Below *One of the popular cars produced by Benz in Germany, in 1899.*

Right *A German steel plant equipped with modern machinery and the latest methods of production.*

The railway

In the summer of 1865 Dickens and a friend left Paris to travel to London by train. After a smooth Channel crossing they were soon travelling through Kent at a comfortable 80 kilometres an hour (50 mph), when suddenly the passengers were flung from their seats. The train had left the track and plunged down an embankment. Dickens, who luckily was unhurt, had been involved in one of the early railway accidents.

The first railway line, which ran between Stockton and Darlington, opened in 1825. In 1829 the engineer George Stephenson built his famous 'Rocket', which won a competition by steaming at 48 kilometres an hour (30 mph). Such a speed seemed unbelievable, for until then no one had travelled faster than the speed of a galloping horse.

Within a few years the country was gripped by a

Below The Rocket.
Right *The introduction of the railways meant that people and goods could be transported much more quickly.*

railway mania. Lines were built to all corners of the land, and by the time of the Great Exhibition they linked London to Dover, Edinburgh, Plymouth and Holyhead. Deep cuttings were carved through the hills, viaducts spanned wide valleys, and rivers which had previously been only crossed by ferry were now passable by bridges.

Passengers and heavy goods were conveyed overnight to destinations which previously would have taken weeks to reach. For the first time poor people from inland towns could visit the seaside. Fresh food was rushed daily into the cities, and new towns, such as Swindon and Crewe, grew up at important railway junctions. Although the motor car was making an appearance by the end of Victoria's reign, the nineteenth century really was the age of the train.

Below and Opposite
Traditional religious beliefs were threatened by Charles Darwin's theories, which proposed that man had evolved naturally from lower forms of life and was closely related to the ape rather than a creation of God.

7 RELIGION, SCIENCE AND CULTURE

Victorian religion

Religion was much more important in Victorian society than it is today. The wealthier classes usually belonged to the Church of England, while poorer believers attended the chapels of Nonconformists, such as Methodists or Baptists. In Ireland and some parts of England, particularly around Liverpool, Roman Catholicism was the dominant faith.

Families often said daily prayers at home, and in the early part of the century most respectable people attended a service on Sundays. In chapels, the sermons were fiery

40

and the singing powerful, while Anglican services, for which the rich had their own reserved family pews, were more restrained.

For much of the Victorian era religious beliefs encouraged a very strict morality among Church-goers. They strongly disapproved of swearing and drinking, divorce was a scandal to them, and they expected clothes to be modest. Ladies were not expected to show more than an ankle beneath their long dresses.

Not all the Victorians, however, were religious. Most of the poor people in the city slums had no time for Church services, because they were more concerned with staying alive. Those who were well-educated began to have doubts about the truth of Christianity, too. New discoveries in the fields of science and history suggested to them that the Bible might not be literal truth. This revelation destroyed the faith of many Christians, and led to a great deal of despair.

Science

Above *Charles Darwin.*

Below *Darwin's ship, HMS* Beagle, *in which he made his worldwide voyage (1831-36).*

Cameras, anaesthetics, dynamite, margarine, torpedoes, refrigerators and light bulbs . . . What do all these have in common? They were all invented during the Victorian era, although not necessarily in Britain. The Victorians were keen scientists, and modern scientific developments have important nineteenth-century roots.

One of the most dramatic scientific theories was proposed by the famous Victorian naturalist, Charles Darwin. After carefully observing plants and animals in different parts of the world, he suggested that different species were not created, but had gradually developed over millions of years. His findings were published in 1859 in *The Origin of Species,* which caused a tremendous sensation. Some people believed that Darwin was undermining Christian teaching about the creation of the world.

The average man or woman, however, would have noticed the developments in medical science more than any work of theory. Two discoveries were particularly exciting. The first was that ether or chloroform made surgical operations painless. Previously, those undergoing surgery had to be either very brave, or very drunk. The second major discovery, made by the Frenchman Louis Pasteur, was of the existence of bacteria (germs). This led to the development of antiseptics, and consequently to a major improvement in the health of the nation.

A vast number of inventions followed upon the Victorian pioneer work in elecricity. Motor cars used electric spark plugs; telegraphs, telephones, wirelesses, electric lighting — all these and other essential gadgets of modern life were the inventions of the inquisitive Victorians.

Right, above *Guglielmo Marconi (1874-1937), the inventor of wireless telegraphy, pictured in 1901 with one of his transmitters.*
Right *The arrest of Dr Crippen, a notorious murderer, following a wireless message relayed from the S S Montrose that informed New Scotland Yard of his presence onboard.*

Above *Thomas Hardy.*

The Arts

The Victorians were avid readers. At the times when we sit down and watch television nowadays, they would probably have picked up a book. The art of novel writing flourished during the Victorian era and this produced some of the finest writers in the English tradition within a relatively short period of time.

As we have seen, Dickens's work was the most popular. Towards the end of the century Thomas Hardy, another author still widely read today, wrote a series of books in which he spoke about human relationships more openly than had been done before. But after the publication of *Jude the Obscure*, in 1895, there was such an outcry that he stopped writing novels. Some modern readers prefer

Right *Crowds flock to the Royal Albert Hall, which was built in the years 1867-71.*

the more restrained novels of Anthony Trollope or George Eliot to the dramatic styles of Dickens and Hardy. George Eliot was, in fact a woman, Mary Ann Evans, but she felt that readers would take her more seriously if she wrote under a man's name.

Much Victorian music, poetry, painting and architecture was sentimental in mood. Railway stations were built like medieval cathedrals, while the songs which families sang round the piano told of broken hearts or returning travellers.

Victorian Britain was constantly changing. What was one day a quiet meadow became a roaring city the next. No one was sure what the future held. Perhaps the sentimentality of their arts compensated the Victorians for the pace of the changing and uncertain world around them.

Above *George Eliot.*

Education

Above *In* Nicholas Nickleby, *the foul and unnourishing food served at mealtimes at Dotheboys Hall, symbolized the kind of education the boys received.*

In 1837, a report was produced which revealed that in many towns only one in twelve children attended school each day. This was not because they played truant, but because they did not have to go to school. There were not enough schools for them anyway. Children of middle-class parents went to private schools and the very wealthy often had tutors. In some areas there were charitable schools for the poor, such as the Ragged Schools which Dickens supported, but their standards were often wretchedly low. Sunday school provided the only education received by most boys and girls.

Slowly, politicians realized that they had to improve the situation. How could the working man be expected to vote wisely if he were not educated? And the new machinery in factories and workshops needed skilled labour to operate and maintain it.

The 1870 Education Act set up School Boards, each equipped with powers to establish elementary schools in areas where they were needed. School attendance was made compulsory in 1880, and free in 1891. These reforms dealt with primary education only. Secondary schools were still fee-paying, and beyond the means of most working-class families. Universities were even more difficult to enter. Although new universities were founded (for example Liverpool in 1882), by 1900 there were only about 20,000 students, of whom very few were women. The terrible schools of Dickens's day might have gone, but by the end of the century the British were still generally not well-educated.

Right *One of the 'Ragged Schools', which were set up to educate those who were too poor to attend even the common day-schools.*

Entertainment

Before about 1850 there was little organized entertainment for the Victorian working class. While wealthier families attended music halls and fairs, many people could look forward to little more than an evening in the local pub, where they drank and sang songs to forget the hardship of their lives. By the end of the century, however, better pay, more holidays, Bank Holidays, and free Saturday afternoons gave them greater opportunities to enjoy seaside holidays or football matches.

At home the middle class relaxed by singing, reading or playing cards. Sometimes they went to a concert or the theatre. The invention of bicycles and the development of railways made people more mobile, enabling them to visit distant relatives or places of interest. Race meetings, especially at Epsom, were great occasions that attracted men and women from all walks of life. They took hampers of food with them and were entertained by a variety of performers and tricksters, as well as by the racing.

Organized sport developed quickly during the Victorian era. Boxing, rugby, tennis, cricket, golf and soccer all took the form that we recognize today. The first F.A. Cup competition took place in 1871 and the Cricket County Championship started in 1873. Women's sport also flourished, although players still had to wear ridiculously long dresses.

Above *The entertainments offered at a Bank Holiday fair held in 1852.*

Left *By the end of the century, a trip to the seaside was a common leisure pursuit for town and city dwellers.*

Right *The music-hall became very popular in the late nineteenth century.*

8 THE EMPIRE AND FOREIGN AFFAIRS

The Empire

Below *The extent of the British Empire in 1900:*
1 Canada; 2 Bahamas and Bermuda; 3 British Guiana; 4 Gambia; 5 Sierra Leone; 6 Gold Coast; 7 Nigeria; 8 Rhodesia, Bechuanaland, South Africa; 9 British East Africa, Uganda, Sudan; 10 Somali; 11 Arabia; 12 India, Burma, Ceylon; 13 Malaya, Sarawak, Brunei; 14 Papua; 15 Australia; 16 Tasmania; 17 New Zealand; 18 Falklands.

During the Victorian period Britain ruled the largest empire the world had ever seen. It was known as the empire on which 'the sun never sets', because it contained countries in all parts of the world. Although it was night-time in London, the sun would be shining on the Union Jack as it flew over the Governor's residence in Ceylon, Hong Kong, or Jamaica. By 1914, the British Empire covered a quarter of the world's land surface and had a population approaching 400 million people.

In 1876, Disraeli gave the Queen the title 'Empress of

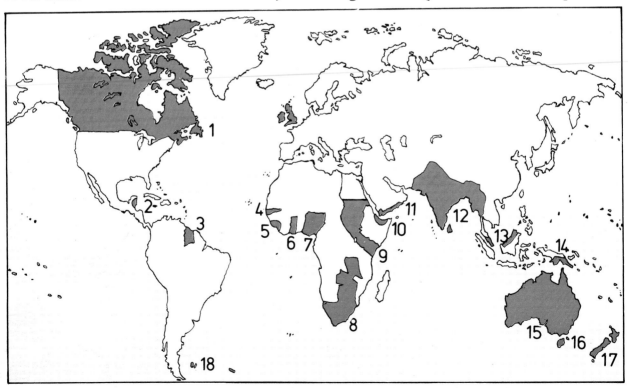

India'. India was the largest of the colonies and was known as the 'Jewel in the Crown'. The Indians themselves, however, had little say in their own government. In countries which had been directly settled from Europe the situation was different. On 1st January 1901, for example, Australia became a self-governing dominion.

Most Victorians were proud of the empire. Its member countries bought British manufactured goods and also supplied the mother country with raw materials, such as tea and rubber. Millions emigrated to the colonies during the nineteenth century, particularly to Canada, New Zealand, Australia and South Africa. Many others went overseas as civil servants, soldiers, explorers or missionaries. Most of the empire was seized by military conquest, and much that the British did in the colonies was unjust. Nevertheless, it was through the tireless efforts of Victorian pioneers that railways and schools were built and modern medicine introduced in some of the remotest regions of the world.

Below *Britain's colonization of foreign countries resulted in the conversion to Christianity of many native populations.*

Britain and Europe

Below *Lord Palmerston.*

Britain avoided fighting a major war in Europe during the Victorian era. For the first part of the nineteenth century she was accepted as the most powerful nation on earth. She dominated world trade, while her massive navy ruled the oceans. The politician who best reflected this age of confident supremacy was Lord Palmerston.

Palmerston held office as either Foreign Secretary or Prime Minister almost continuously between 1830 and 1865. He bullied the Chinese into war in 1839 and 1856, forced the Greeks to give way to British might in 1850, and he interfered continually in other countries' affairs. In 1861 he almost involved Britain in the American Civil War. However, the most serious conflict in which British forces were engaged during this time was the Crimean War of 1854-56.

Above *The 'Charge of the Light Brigade' during the Crimean War, which was immortalized in a poem by Alfred Lord Tennyson.*

For a long time the power of the Turkish Empire in the Eastern Mediterranean had been declining. Britain, France and Austria were worried that Russia would take Turkey's place as the dominant power in the area. It was to prevent a Russian advance that the Crimean War was fought. Disraeli threatened war again in 1878 for similar reasons but managed to negotiate a peace treaty.

By the last years of the century the political map of Europe had changed. After 1871 Germany emerged as a new power, able to challenge Britain's position in the colonies, in the market place and even on the high seas. By the start of the twentieth century statesmen were feeling that the long era of peace could not last very much longer.

9 THE VICTORIAN AGE

Never before had so many changes taken place in Britain in so short a time as occurred in the Victorian age. Towns, railways, monuments and docks were built almost overnight. New ideas and inventions abounded. Science promised to answer all questions as men explored the remotest corners of our planet and even dreamed of flying to the moon. Nothing seemed impossible to the Victorians.

The age was one of dramatic contrasts. It was a time of strong religious faith, but also one during which most people stopped going regularly to church. Britain had never been wealthier, yet at least a third of the population lived in extreme poverty.

Much of our life today rests upon foundations laid in the last century. Our technology is based upon their discoveries, as is modern medicine. Wherever we look, we are in debt to our Victorian ancestors. No one captured the spirit of the age better than Charles Dickens. In his stories we find side by side the squalor and the wealth, the humour and the misery, the old and new, hope and despair. All is drawn with such sympathy, vivid colour and energy, that the Victorian age remains as alive as ever.

Opposite *Some inventions and achievements of the Victorian Age: Brunel's S S Great Britain (1843); the first cross-channel flight by balloon (1882); Fox-Talbot's camera and negatives (1835); Croydon telephone exchange (1884).*

Right Derby Day *by William Frith, a painting which reflects the vitality of the Victorians.*

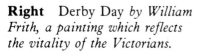

Table of dates

1812 Dickens was born at Landport.

1815 Battle of Waterloo ends the wars against Napoleon.

1824 Dickens works at Warren's Blacking Factory.

1825 Stockton-Darlington railway opened.

1829 George Stephenson builds the 'Rocket'.

1832 Great Reform Act. Dickens becomes a Parliamentary reporter.

1836-37 Dickens publishes *The Pickwick Papers*.

1837-38 Accession of Victoria. Dickens publishes *Oliver Twist*.

1842 Mines Act. Dickens's first visit to America.

1843 Dickens publishes *A Christmas Carol*.

1846 Repeal of The Corn Laws, which allows cheap foreign corn to enter Britain.

1848 Last Chartist Movement. Public Health Act.

1849-50 Dickens publishes *David Copperfield*.

1851 Great Exhibition.

1854-56 Crimean War.

1858 Dickens begins tour of public readings.

1859 Darwin's *Origin of Species* published.

1860-61 Dickens publishes *Great Expectations*.

1861 Prince Albert dies.

1867 Second Reform. Lister uses carbolic antiseptic.

1870 Secret Ballot Act. Dickens dies at Gadshill.

1875 Public Health Act. Artisans Dwellings Act.

1884 Third Reform Act.

1888 Local Government Act.

1889 London Dock Strike.

1891 Hardy publishes *Tess of the D'Urbervilles*.

1895 Hardy publishes *Jude the Obscure*.

1900 Labour Party formed.

1901 Death of Queen Victoria.

Glossary

Aristocrat   Titled person from the upper class.

Blacking   Black colouring for leather.

Bribe   Money given to influence someone.

Capital Punishment   The death penalty, as a punishment for a serious crime.

Civil Servant   Someone who works for the Government.

Constituency   Area represented in Parliament by a Member of Parliament.

Convict   Person found guilty of a crime.

Democracy   Society in which every adult has the vote.

Electorate   The people of a country who are permitted to vote.

Emigrate   To leave a country in order to live permanently in another country.

Export   To sell goods to a foreign country.

Humane   Kind; merciful; sympathetic.

Import   To bring goods into a country.

Missionary   Person who tries to spread a religious faith in other countries.

Music hall   Theatre for light entertainment.

Nationalist   One who puts his nation first.

Nonconformist   Member of a Protestant church, other than the Church of England.

Novel   A long story, usually a work of fiction.

Slum   Very poor housing.

Slump   Sudden economic collapse.

Tutor   Personal teacher.

Viaduct   Long bridge built on many pillars, crossing from one side of a valley to another, for example.

Further information

Books

Dawes, Penelope, *Children of the Industrial Revolution* (Wayland 1972)

Ferguson, Sheila, *Growing Up in Victorian Britain* (Batsford 1977)

Fido, Martin, *Charles Dickens* (Hamlyn 1970)

Harrison, Molly, *Growing Up in Victorian England* (Wayland 1980)

Hill, C. P. and Wright, J. C., *British History 1815-1914* (Oxford 1981)

Huggett, Frank E., *A Day in the Life of a Victorian Farm Worker* (Allen & Unwin 1972)

Huggett, Frank E., *A Day in the Life of a Victorian Factory Worker* (Allen & Unwin 1973)

Margetson, Stella, *Victorian People* (Batsford 1977)

Quennell, Marjorie and C. H. B., *A History of Everyday Things in England*, Vols III and IV (Batsford 1961)

Parker, M. St. J., and Reid, D. J., *The British Revolution* (Blandford 1972)

Reader, W. J., *Victorian England* (Batsford, 1974)

Rooke, Patrick, *The Age of Dickens* (Wayland 1972)

Rooke, Patrick, *Gladstone and Disraeli* (Wayland 1970)

Scott, Alastair, *One Day in Victorian England* (Tyndall 1974)

Williams-Ellis, Annabel, and Stubbs, William, *Victorian England* (Blackie 1969)

Places to visit

Museums Your local museum is likely to have a number of exhibits relating to Victorian Britain, but you will find the famous London Museums even better. Try to visit the Victoria and Albert Museum and the Science Museum. In Madame Tussard's Waxworks you can see models of famous Victorians, while excellent portraits of them can be found in the National Portrait Gallery.

Famous sites Victorian architecture is still all around us, in houses, shops, railway stations and lines, bridges and other buildings. Some of the more famous examples are the Albert Hall and St. Pancras Station in London. Many places mentioned in Dickens's novels still exist and you can see his birthplace in Landport, Portsmouth.

Libraries All libraries stock Dickens's books, as well as plenty of other material on the Victorian age.

Index

Picture Acknowledgements

The illustrations in this book were supplied by: The Mansell Collection 17, 22, 32, 36 (top), 42 (top); The Mary Evans Picture Library 6 (bottom), 8, 10, 12 (bottom), 19 (top), 24 (top), 26 (bottom), 28, 31 (bottom), 44, 45, 46, 52; other illustrations are from the Wayland Picture Library.